Animal Habitats

The Eagle in the Mountains

Text by Jim Scott

Photographs by
Wendy Shattil & Bob Rozinski
Oxford Scientific Films

Gareth Stevens Publishing
Milwaukee

Contents

Note: The use of capital letters for an eagle's name indicates that it is a *species* of eagle (for example, Bald Eagle). The use of a lowercase, or small, letter means that it is a member of the larger *group* of eagles.

A majestic Bald Eagle soars above its mountain home.

Perched on a snowy branch, a Bald Eagle scans the winter landscape of North America.

Where eagles live

Eagles are the largest of all the birds of *prey*. They can be seen, soaring through the skies, in many parts of the world, from the hot jungles of the tropics to the snow-covered lands of the north.

One reason eagles are so widespread is their ability to fly long distances. Over the ages, different kinds of eagles have come to live in certain places. Some have chosen the mountains, while others live in woodlands. Eagles also inhabit grasslands, deserts, and the coasts of oceans. Most eagles prefer to live far from people, in wild, remote countryside.

As birds of prey, eagles eat other birds, fish, snakes, and small mammals, like rabbits and squirrels. Eagles are well known for their hunting ability and usually eat whatever food is most abundant. Their keen eyesight and powerful flight have helped to make them *extremely effective predators.*

Eagles spend their days flying, perching on cliffs or in trees, and hunting. At night they usually roost in trees, resting and sleeping. When the seasons change, eagles often travel from one area to another. These movements usually depend on their food supply. Eagles in the northern mountains often fly south in the autumn, returning north each spring to breed. The birds may travel hundreds of miles on these journeys, which are called *migrations.*

Because of their enormous size and incredible powers of flight, eagles are some of the most impressive birds on Earth. They are also among the most beautiful of birds. Few sights compare to the majestic eagle, soaring high over the mountains.

The family of booted eagles includes the beautiful Golden Eagle. These birds have thick feathers on their legs.

Eagles around the world

There are about 60 species of eagles living around the world. Different kinds of eagles have become adapted to different regions and lifestyles. The eagles of the world are usually divided into four main groups.

Among the best-known are the sea eagles. These large birds usually live near water and feed on fish. They often feed together, gathering in places where fish are abundant. The American Bald Eagle is one of the most easily recognizable of the sea eagles. They are big birds, with a wingspan of 6 ft (2 m) or more. They can be identified by their white heads, brown bodies, and white tail feathers. Bald Eagles are not really bald at all. The word "bald" comes from the Old English word "balde," meaning white. Several other sea eagles, including the African Fish Eagle, also have white heads.

The snake eagles, like this Black-breasted Snake Eagle, have bright yellow eyes.

The booted eagles are the world's largest group of eagles. They are named after the thick covering of feathers on their legs, which look a bit like boots or trousers. The Golden Eagle, found in North America, Britain, Europe, and Asia, is probably the most common type of booted eagle. Golden Eagles are large brown birds about the size of Bald Eagles. They have a heavy coat of dark feathers on their legs. These eagles often fly over mountains, woodlands, and grasslands — using their sharp eyesight to spot small mammals. A close cousin of the Golden Eagle, the Steppe Eagle, ranges from central Europe to the Soviet Union, Africa, and India.

The snake eagles form another group of eagles. Just as one would expect, they often feed on snakes and other reptiles. Most snake eagles are found in Europe, Asia, and Africa. The European Snake Eagle is the best known of all the snake eagles. Snake eagles vary in size, depending on the species, but all snake eagles have strong, stubby toes, which they use to grasp the bodies of snakes. They have bright yellow eyes, with which they scan the ground from perches or cliffs. Snake eagles live in open deserts, woodlands, and tropical forests, where they often catch snakes — and swallow them headfirst.

Harpy eagles form the last group. These powerful birds are extremely large and beautifully colored. They usually live in tropical jungles. One species in this group, the South American Harpy Eagle, often feeds on monkeys and other jungle animals.

African Fish Eagles are well adapted for living along coastlines. They closely resemble Bald Eagles in appearance and behavior.

A Bateleur, found in Africa. This magnificent member of the snake eagle family prefers to prey on mammals.

Lofty peaks rising in the distance form a stunning backdrop for these perching Bald Eagles.

Eagles in the mountains

Eagles inhabit mountain ranges in every corner of the world. They can be found from the smallest hillocks in Britain to the towering Himalayan Mountains of Asia, which rise to a height of 29,000 ft (almost 9,000 m). In every mountain range over which they soar, eagles make the most of the available food supplies below.

Mountain *habitats* vary considerably from place to place. The upper parts are often bare and rocky and frequently covered with snow. Below this comes the barren *tundra* or alpine grassland, while lower still may be broad forests, alpine meadows, lush valleys, or deep river gorges. The vertical distance between the foothills rising out of the plains to the alpine tundra far above the tree line may be several miles. Within that range live a wide variety of animals and plants, each adapted to particular conditions.

Eagles may live in different areas in the mountains at different times of the year. Since some of their food sources, like deer, wild sheep, and goats, migrate up and down the mountains seasonally, eagles tend to move in a similar way. Deer may live near the alpine tundra in the warm summer months, eating the abundant grasses and mosses that grow above the tree line. During the harsh winters, however, deer migrate down the mountainside to avoid the deep snows and to find accessible grasses and herbs. Eagles searching for deer also move down from high altitudes in the cold winter months. They scan the lower regions of the foothills and plains from the air or from perches like trees and cliffs.

At high altitudes, smaller mammals, such as rabbits, hares, and squirrels, may hibernate during the cold mountain winters. The disappearance of these small creatures, which move into snug burrows, also causes eagles to move lower down the mountains in search of food.

During winter, the high mountain lakes and rivers freeze over. Waterfowl such as ducks and geese, which eagles like to prey on, are forced to move south to milder climates. Frozen water also makes the fish unavailable to the eagles until the mild spring weather returns.

Because of their incredible powers of flight, eagles enjoy the luxury of scouting far and wide for food. If need be, they can move many miles a day, and hundreds of miles over the course of a season. In winter, snow, wind, and extremely cold conditions turn the high mountains into empty and silent places. In spring, however, when the ice melts and the mammals emerge from their dens or return from migrations, the eagles return to hunt for prey on the heights.

Evergreen forests are favorite haunts of Golden Eagles.

An eagle's sharp beak is well adapted for tearing and swallowing prey.

The eagle's body

The largest eagles may weigh up to 12 lbs (5.4 kg) and have a wingspan of up to 8 ft (2.4 m). The wings of different species of eagles vary in shape. Eagles that live in the forest usually have shorter wings, allowing them to maneuver around branches and other tight places. Eagles that live in open areas generally have longer wings that make soaring and gliding easier.

All eagles have sharp eyesight. Their eyes are believed to be about eight times as powerful as our own. Golden Eagles can spot a rabbit running from more than 2 miles (3.2 km) away. Bald Eagles can see a fish in water from about 1/2 mile (0.8 km) away. Eagles also have a good sense of hearing. This allows them to listen for the calls of other eagles, which may be far away.

Eagles catch and kill prey with the *talons* on their feet. Talons are large claws that are well suited to hunting. The feet of different eagle species vary according to their lifestyle. Fish-eating eagles have *spicules* on the soles of their toes. These spicules are actually small hooks or barbs that help the bird grasp slippery fish. Golden Eagles have very strong hind claws to grasp and carry small mammals. This hind claw is the largest of an eagle's four claws.

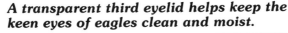

A transparent third eyelid helps keep the keen eyes of eagles clean and moist.

Eagles have eyesight about eight times as powerful as our own.

By flexing their leg muscles, eagles can close their talons. This helps them grab and hold on to prey, and cling to branches when resting or sleeping.

Eagles have large hooked beaks for killing prey and tearing at flesh. They don't chew their food. Their large mouths let them swallow big pieces of meat. Eagles often store food in their *crop* after swallowing it. The crop is a pouchlike sack in the gullet. Eagles can store up to 2 lbs (1 kg) of food in their crop, which allows them to gorge themselves when food is abundant. You can often tell if an eagle has been feeding by the bulge in its throat.

Female eagles are larger than males. Young eagles are plainly colored and do not acquire their brighter adult *plumage* for several years. The coloring of adult eagles probably helps the birds communicate. Adults recognize each other by their plumage during the breeding season, and this helps them select a mate. Once a year eagles lose their feathers and grow new ones. This process, which happens gradually during the summer months, is called *molting*. Eagles don't lose their feathers all at once, so they are always able to fly during their molt.

Eagles use their strong talons to grasp branches while resting and sleeping. They are also used for grabbing and killing prey.

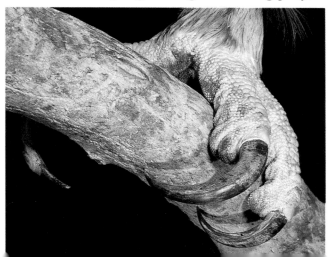

9

The lightweight feathers of eagles change color as the bird matures.

A Bald Eagle takes off from a snowfield in Alaska. The wing slots on the tips of their wings help these birds maneuver in the air.

Flight and migration

The wings of eagles are well adapted for soaring and gliding. These birds seem to float effortlessly on the currents of warm air that rise from the ground to form *thermals* in the sky. Eagles also search for updrafts of air created by wind blowing over hillsides and mountains. These updrafts can sometimes carry them for long distances. When flying at lower altitudes or taking off from a perch, eagles have to maintain a steady flapping of their wings to stay aloft. This kind of flight seems to involve a lot of hard work compared with soaring and gliding!

Wing slots at the ends of their wings enable eagles to twist and turn in the sky. These wing slots are actually gaps between the feathers that help eagles adjust their movements in the air. Eagles also tilt their tail feathers back and forth to help them steer, much like the rudder of a ship. Like most birds, eagles have strong, lightweight skeletons that make flying much easier. Bird skeletons weigh very little because their bones are hollow.

Eagles may fly many miles in a day searching for food. They almost always use air currents and updrafts to make these searches easier. Bald Eagles often fly over mountain lakes or along coastlines, looking for fish, waterfowl, and other food. Golden Eagles fly over mountains or open country, searching for small mammals.

Bald Eagles are well known for their long-distance migrations each autumn and spring.

When the seasons change, many eagles move on to other places. Some seem to move at random in response to the weather or the need for food. Others have traditional migration routes that take them to the same places year after year. Generally, eagles move to avoid harsh, cold winters that may limit food supplies. The distances vary greatly according to species. Golden Eagles may only move a few miles from the mountains to the plains, while Bald Eagles sometimes travel hundreds of miles in their search for milder climates and open water.

Most Bald Eagles travel south in the autumn, returning north in the spring. Migrating Bald Eagles may travel over a hundred miles (160 km) a day. They usually journey in the afternoons, when the air has warmed up enough to create updrafts. If it is raining or snowing, eagles will usually stop and wait for better weather. They usually fly alone, feeding along the way, but often join up with other eagles at their final destination.

Eagles often search for currents of warm air rising from the ground to keep them aloft.

Gulls often join eagles in feeding on the abundant salmon that spawn in Alaska each autumn.

Food and feeding

Eagles eat many different kinds of food, including rabbits, birds, snakes, and fish. They also eat *carrion*, which is the dead flesh of animals. Eagles take advantage of nature by eating whatever is most plentiful in the areas where they live.

Eagles living near water feed mainly on fish. Fish-eating eagles like the Bald Eagle cruise rivers and coastlines looking for salmon. These birds may dive from great heights to snatch a wriggling salmon from the water. They carry the salmon, some weighing several pounds, to a nearby perch to eat. During the salmon runs, when the swarms of fish are moving upriver to lay their eggs, scores of eagles can be seen circling over particular stretches of rivers. Fish eagles also eat shad, herring, catfish, and carp.

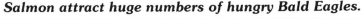

Salmon attract huge numbers of hungry Bald Eagles.

12

Bald Eagles have sometimes been observed stealing food from other birds. They frequently take fish from the Osprey, a fish hawk that lives in many of the same places. Bald Eagles will chase Ospreys, forcing them to drop the fish they have caught. Then the eagle will grab the fish, sometimes in midair, and carry it to a nearby perch to feast.

Eagles also prey on water birds, such as ducks and geese. They may seek out birds that are weak or crippled and, therefore, easier to catch. Among the favorite foods of Golden Eagles are rabbits and rodents. These soaring birds of the mountains and plains use their keen eyesight to spot their prey, diving from high in the sky onto the unlucky victim. Having caught the animal in its talons, the eagle then tears at the flesh with its strong, hooked bill. Small mammals are easily immobilized by an eagle's strong talons, which can pierce their bodies and crush small bones.

Bald Eagles living by the ocean often eat the dead bodies of beached seals, whales, and other marine mammals that have been washed ashore. Sometimes dozens of eagles can be seen feeding on a single carcass. Eagles living further inland may eat the carcasses of deer and elk that have died during harsh winters.

Eagles don't usually feed every day. By feasting when food is plentiful, they can survive for several weeks without eating when there is little food around. If food supplies in a certain area dwindle too much, eagles simply move to another place to feed. Like most birds of prey, eagles regurgitate pellets after feeding. These pellets are made up of indigestible food, such as fur, feathers, and bones. The pellets pass from the gizzard to the mouth, where they are cast out.

Successful eagles often carry unlucky fish to nearby perches, where they are devoured.

Eagles in winter

During the long winters, some eagles gather in groups to live. This gathering of eagles in winter is a spectacular sight. Bald Eagles usually fly south, but some may travel east or west to coastal regions of open water. They often reach their destinations as early as November and stay until March.

The greatest wintering concentrations of Bald Eagles occur in January and February. At times, hundreds or even thousands of birds can be seen together in the coastal mountain areas, roosting in trees, feeding, soaring, or bathing. The eagles generally return to the same wintering grounds year after year.

Eagles winter in areas where food is abundant. In some parts of North America, Bald Eagles often congregate along rivers and lakes which are full of fish. In Canada and Alaska, the birds seem to prefer areas along the Pacific Coast, where there is a milder climate, open water, and a wealth of spawning salmon. Bald Eagles are frequently spotted along the shorelines of rivers and coastlines, eating dead and dying fish.

The Chilkat River in Alaska has the largest concentration of wintering Bald Eagles in the world. More than 3,000 of them come to the Chilkat region each autumn to feed on salmon running up the river. Part of the Chilkat River and the surrounding area has now been set aside as a refuge for the birds, so that logging and other industries nearby will not disturb the eagles or destroy their habitat.

The roosting of Bald Eagles in winter is a spectacular sight. These birds may return to the same winter roosts year after year.

Hundreds of Bald Eagles may share the same roosting area. They may also feed, soar, and bathe together.

To save energy, eagles spend most winter days perching quietly in trees. They may venture out to feed in the morning, gathering in groups when food is discovered. They sometimes follow other local birds to favorite feeding sites. When the temperatures rise in the afternoons, the eagles can be seen soaring together on thermals high in the air. At night, they roost together in nearby trees. These roosts, which are used year after year, may contain several hundred birds.

Eagles often establish first contact with each other during the mating season by calling from their perches.

Courtship and mating

Eagles usually begin breeding when they are between three and six years old. This is about the time they attain their adult plumage. As juveniles, Bald Eagles have a mottled brown and white appearance, while Golden Eagles are uniformly dark brown with white patches on the wings and tail feathers. Between three and four years of age, both species acquire their true adult coloration. Bald Eagles now have white head and tail feathers, while the wing and tail feathers of the Golden Eagles have turned a rich brown. This adult plumage is a signal to other eagles that the birds are ready to breed.

During the early spring the adult eagles select a mate. This is called "pair bonding," and is similar to human marriage. Once they have made their choice, most eagles remain with the same mate year after year.

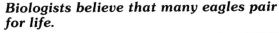

Biologists believe that many eagles pair for life.

A pair of Bald Eagles perches on a conspicuous branch, warning other eagles to stay away.

The courtship of eagles is one of the most beautiful of all wildlife spectacles. They often establish the first contact by calling to each other from perches or while soaring. Courting eagles also chase each other through the air, zigzagging, diving, and soaring high over the mountain landscape. At times one of the birds may fly upside down and grab the talons of its mate. Both birds will then roll over together in midair. They may also dive together from a great height, pulling up at the last second before they reach the ground. They then rise swiftly into the air again and repeat the performance. This is known as "roller coastering."

The best-known eagle courtship display is called "cartwheeling." The birds first climb high into the sky and lock their talons, then spin and spiral down toward the earth. Eagles often perform their displays above mountain ridges, where rising air currents help them perform acrobatic maneuvers. They may concentrate on a single display or combine a number of different displays in their aerial performances.

A pair of breeding eagles will chase other eagles away from their *territory* in the mountains. They often warn other eagles to keep away by calling at them in high-pitched tones or perching in noticeable places. Eagle pairs will also circle high over intruding birds, which is another way of warning the unwelcome guests to leave. This aggressive behavior greatly benefits the pairing eagles. It allows them to mate, rear young, and hunt for food in relative peace and quiet, with little competition from other birds.

Nesting and laying eggs

After mating, the eagles concentrate on building their nest. Most eagles build enormous nests. One of the reasons they are so large is that eagles usually repair and add to them year after year. The nests are usually built in a prominent place with a good view of the surrounding countryside — in sturdy trees, on cliffs or ledges, or even on the ground. Eagles usually build their nests with large sticks which they weave together like a basket. This helps to support the weight of the birds. One Bald Eagle's nest in the United States weighed nearly 2 tons — about the weight of a small car!

Eagles' nests may be shaped like bowls or upside-down cones, while some may have only a slight depression in the center for the eggs. Eagles often place grasses, pine needles, and feathers in the middle of the nest to provide a soft resting place for the eggs. The birds also bring green branches to place into their nests. Although these branches may seem like pretty decoration, they are more likely to be signals to other eagles that the nest is occupied.

Eagles often build more than one nest, although only one is used for laying eggs. They often have two or three nests in their territory, and one Golden Eagle pair was known to have as many as fourteen different nests!

Eagle nests are most often found in trees and on cliffs. These birds often rebuild them year after year.

Resembling huge baskets, eagle nests are usually woven together with large sticks.

Some biologists think that eagles make several nests in case one is destroyed. Others think that the extra nests may advertise, to other eagles, the fact that the territory is occupied. Scientists also think that the eagles avoid *parasites*, such as lice, by moving periodically to a different nest. By building or rebuilding their nests together each year, the pair bond between the mating eagles is strengthened. Most of the nest building is done in the spring, although the two birds may work on their nests over the course of several seasons. It may take them up to a month to construct a new nest.

Sturdy as they are, eagle nests are sometimes destroyed by severe weather. Eagles will often rebuild their damaged nests if it is still early in the breeding season. However, they may abandon their nests when disturbed by humans even if eggs have been laid.

Eagles may lay between one and four eggs, but most often the *clutch* consists of just two. The eggs are generally laid at intervals of two to four days. If the eggs are removed from the nests by predators or through an accident, the female will sometimes lay a new clutch.

Pine needles and grasses are often placed in nests by eagles. This provides a soft resting place for eggs and young alike.

Young eagles usually hatch at intervals of two to three days.

Incubation and hatching

Both eagle parents take turns sitting on the eggs to keep them warm. This is called *incubation*. The male brings food to the nest for the female, who spends more of the time incubating the eggs. Like many birds, eagles have a *"brood patch"* on their breasts that helps keep the eggs warm. This bare patch on the skin has few feathers, but many blood vessels. It comes into close contact with the eggs when the bird sits on the nest.

Eagles rarely leave their eggs unattended. If the female leaves to feed, the male takes over the incubation. If the eggs are left alone, even for a minute, the parent will often cover them with soft nesting material to keep them warm. This also hides the fragile eggs from predators such as crows and ravens.

The parents turn their eggs over periodically so that they are evenly warmed. This ensures that the *embryo* develops properly inside the shell. When the incubating adult wants to leave the nest, it calls to its mate as a signal. The other parent then comes to the nest and takes over. When eagles switch positions, the arriving parent may pull nesting material up around its body to help protect the eggs. The length of the incubation period varies from species to species. Bald Eagle eggs usually take about 35 days to hatch, while Golden Eagle eggs may take at least 40 days or more.

A helpless Golden Eagle chick investigates its new surroundings. This nest is lined with the fur of rodents.

Just before hatching, the chicks can be heard cheeping from inside the eggshells. Now they must break out from the shells in order to get air to breathe. Hatching may take only a few hours, or sometimes up to two days. The chicks cut their way out of the shell with their sharp "egg tooth," a small projection on the end of the beak. They use this egg tooth like a chisel, cutting a ring around the eggshell before pushing the shell apart.

Each tiny eaglet emerges from the shell wet and helpless, with its eyes closed. The eaglets are very weak at first and can barely raise their heads. Within hours, however, the silky *down* covering their bodies dries out and they open their eyes. The first day is usually spent sleeping and recovering from the tiring business of hatching. By the second day the parents are placing small pieces of meat into the beaks of their offspring.

Newly hatched Golden and Bald Eagle chicks weigh only about 3 oz (85 g). But after the first few days, they soon put on weight and begin to grow. If there is more than one egg in the nest, the young hatch at intervals of two to three days. This means that the first chick to hatch is bigger and stronger than the rest. This older, stronger chick may attack and kill the others, especially when food is scarce. This is nature's way of ensuring that at least one of the chicks survives to continue the species.

This newly hatched Golden Eagle chick will be fed by its parents for several months.

Nearing their first independent flight, these young Golden Eagles await a delivery of food from their parents.

Growing up

After the eggs have hatched, the parents are kept very busy caring for their chicks. The young continually beg for food, and the parents spend more and more time hunting over the lofty mountain peaks. The young eaglets soon learn how to take slivers of meat from the beaks of the adults.

As with many birds, eagles are said to *fledge* when they leave the nest and make their first independent flight. The first stage of their development toward fledging is known as the "downy stage." The silky white down, which covers the eaglet's body from birth, remains on the eaglet for its first three to five weeks. During this time the parents must protect the young birds from the sun, rain, and strong winds.

This first downy coat eventually disappears and is replaced by a second, woolen coat of down. After a few more weeks these young birds enter the feathering stage. Now, feathers begin to pop up on their backs, breasts, shoulders, and wings. By this time, the eaglets have become more skilled at taking food from their parents. They begin to try feeding themselves from meat scraps that have been dropped into the nest.

An immature eagle finally attains true flight.

The last stage of development before fledging is known as the "feathered stage." By about eight weeks of age, the eaglets are covered with true feathers, although they still cannot fly. During this period they often *preen* themselves, stroking their bodies with their bills to remove old feathers and make room for new ones. Their beaks and talons grow quickly now, in preparation for the hunting skills they will soon need. The parents begin to leave the nest for longer periods, returning only to deliver food. Now the eaglets spend most of their time sleeping, eating, and lounging in the sun.

Once the true feathers have grown in, though, at about ten weeks of age, the young eaglets are almost ready to fly. They often hop from branch to branch, stretching their wings in readiness for their upcoming flights. They generally fledge without any coaxing from their parents. This fledging may only be a short flight to another branch, or it could be a full-blown journey from their mountain nest down a nearby valley.

After fledging, the young birds stay in the vicinity of the nest for the rest of the summer, learning to hunt and fend for themselves. The parent birds continue to provide their young with food as they teach them the finer points of hunting. By autumn, the young eagles have reached full independence. Soon they drift away into the skies to begin their own lives.

This young Bald Eagle is now on its own. It will not develop its white head and tail feathers for several years.

Black Bears share the mountains with eagles and many other animals.

A Cottontail Rabbit, ever alert for predators.

Mountain neighbors

Wildlife abounds in the mountains, sharing the varied habitats and scenery with the eagles. Deer and elk wander through forests or on open ground, browsing on grasses and herbs. Squirrels and chipmunks scurry through the trees and across rocky hillsides. Grouse and other ground-nesting birds live among the heather. Small mammals like mice and voles scamper along the ground from hole to hole, feeding on plants. Foxes, weasels, and martens emerge from their dens after dark, searching for these mice and voles to eat for themselves.

Mountains are also home to Black and Grizzly Bears. These bears eat a variety of food, from other mammals to berries, honey, or birds' eggs. Large cats also live in the mountains, hunting during the night. The American Mountain Lion, or Puma, which may weigh up to 200 lbs (90 kg), preys on herds of deer. Smaller cats like the Lynx and Bobcat have smaller appetites. They often stalk through the darkness on silent paws, seeking rabbits and squirrels. Many of these animals, including the wildcats, foxes, weasels, and bears, compete with eagles for the same kind of food.

Eagles share their airspace with a variety of other birds. The mountains are also home to the eagles' smaller cousins, the hawks and falcons. The larger hawks soar and hunt much like eagles, while falcons swoop and dive swiftly after birds and mammals. All these birds of prey use their excellent vision and powers of flight when catching prey.

An unlucky duck has become dinner for this Northern Harrier, a low-flying hawk that cruises the foothills in search of prey.

Smaller birds like jays and crows perch in the trees, cawing noisily. Songbirds flit through the mountain forests, singing from the treetops. Swifts and swallows dart through the air, looking for insects. Other flying insect-eaters, the bats, zip about the mountains, eating mosquitoes and other insects. Mountain bats live together in large caves, hanging upside down and sleeping during the day, only venturing out to feed in the evenings.

Many fish are found in the rivers and lakes of the mountains, including trout and salmon, which are closely related to each other. These silvery fish usually feed on insects, often leaping from the clear water to catch them. Beavers live along mountain streams, damming the water and making their homes with the willow branches they have felled. Muskrats also live in the mountain lakes and rivers, feeding on plants. Mink sometimes prowl the banks of these waters, searching for frogs and crayfish.

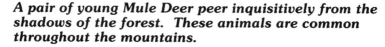

A pair of young Mule Deer peer inquisitively from the shadows of the forest. These animals are common throughout the mountains.

Eagles and people

People have always been fascinated by these magnificent birds of prey. Eagles are often mentioned in songs, fables, and legends, and also in stories in the Bible. Throughout the world, and for thousands of years, these birds have been admired for their power, courage, and strength.

North American Indians worshipped many forms of wildlife, including eagles. Both Bald and Golden Eagles were a part of many Indian ceremonies and rituals. Indians believed that these mysterious birds possessed certain magical powers.

Likenesses of eagles were also carved on totem poles. These totem poles, carved from tree trunks, often featured the likenesses of eagles and other wild animals as symbols of power. The eagle was also a symbol of immortality. Totem poles are still used today by some Indians living in the northwestern United States and western Canada.

Native American peoples sometimes dressed and danced as if they were eagles, and some tribes continue this tradition today. Eagle feathers were often used to decorate war bonnets, spears, shirts, and tomahawks. Because Indians used eagle feathers in their religious ceremonies, these birds were often hunted. The Indians believed they could capture an eagle's

Native American totem poles are often carved with likenesses of eagles. Eagles have long been looked on as symbols of courage and power.

A beaded apron, woven by a member of the Tlingit tribe of Alaska.

spirit by catching or killing the bird. Some Indian tribes even kept eagles in cages, ensuring a constant supply of valuable feathers. These feathers were believed to carry powerful messages. Native Americans also decorated themselves with the bones and talons of eagles. The bones were sometimes used as whistles, and talons were carried as a token of good luck.

Our fascination with the mystery and power of eagles has continued into modern times. The mighty eagle is currently the national emblem of several countries, including the United States, which officially adopted the Bald Eagle as its national emblem in 1782. Pictures of eagles are found on coins, paper money, and the official seals of several nations.

Despite our admiration for eagles, they have been treated badly by humans around the world. Unfortunately, at least twenty species of eagles, including the Bald Eagle, are now considered to be *endangered*. This means that these species are in danger of disappearing from the Earth forever.

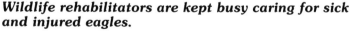

Wildlife rehabilitators are kept busy caring for sick and injured eagles.

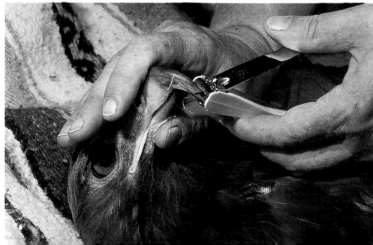

The dangers to eagles

Because they are predators, eagles have few natural enemies. However, their eggs are sometimes stolen and their young attacked and killed in the nest. Unfortunately, the greatest danger to eagles throughout the world comes from people. Eagles have been shot, poisoned, and trapped, and they have had their homes destroyed. Today, the existence of some species of eagles is threatened as a direct result of human activity.

Many eagles have been shot over the past centuries by farmers, herdsmen, gamekeepers, and ranchers who thought eagles were killing their domestic animals. These livestock owners have also set steel traps baited with meat to kill eagles. We know today that, in most cases, eagles were unjustly blamed for this killing. But the slaughter took a heavy toll on eagle populations. In Great Britain, the European Sea Eagle was exterminated from the country in the early 1900s because it was thought to be killing lambs. Many Bald and Golden Eagles in the United States have been shot, trapped, and poisoned during the past two centuries for the same reason.

Artificial poisons have also had a serious effect on eagle populations. During the 1940s and 1950s, *pesticides* like DDT were used all over the world to protect agricultural crops from insects. A great many eagles and other animals were also killed by mistake. After being sprayed onto the land, these pesticides move into the soil and water. The poisons were absorbed into the bodies of birds and fish, so that eagles preying on these animals also took in the poison. The poisons often prevented eagles from reproducing

An injured Golden Eagle is nursed back to health at a wildlife rehabilitation center.

Power lines can be deadly to unsuspecting eagles.

Shrinking habitats are among the greatest perils to eagles. Roads, cities, and other development have invaded pristine wilderness in recent decades.

properly. Many poisoned eagles were unable to lay eggs, while others laid eggs with shells so thin that they broke or failed to hatch.

Another danger from humans comes from the destruction of wildlife habitats in order to build roads, houses, or factories. Vast areas of forest have been cut down or burned, destroying the eagles' territory. We have polluted many rivers and lakes with chemicals, killing the fish and waterfowl that eagles feed on. Many eagles have also been electrocuted by perching on electrical power lines.

But now, at last, many people are trying to save eagles. Shooting and trapping have been outlawed in some countries, and those who break the law are punished with stiff penalties. Some nations, including the United States, have stopped using DDT and other pesticides that were harming eagles and other wild animals. In recent years, some electric companies have been designing power lines that make eagles safe from electrocution.

Rehabilitation centers for injured eagles have also been started in many places. Volunteers at these centers look after sick and injured eagles, nursing them back to health and releasing them into the wild. In areas where eagles have disappeared, wildlife biologists have reintroduced them in an attempt to reestablish populations. But in many countries around the world, the killing of eagles continues.

Life in the mountains

Like many other predators, eagles come at the top of their food chain. It is through food chains that energy flows up from plants to animals, and finally back to the earth. At the bottom of the food chain are water and land plants, which get their energy from the sun and from *nutrients* in the soil and water. These plants are eaten by a variety of animals, including insects, small fish, birds, rodents, deer, and elk. Eagles and other predators at the top of the food chain feed on these fish, birds, and mammals. When all these living things die, their bodies break down and *decompose*. Some may be eaten by other animals, but eventually the nutrients are returned to the water and soil to be used again by other plants and animals. These food chains, which carry energy in a large circle, are vital to all living things.

Food chain

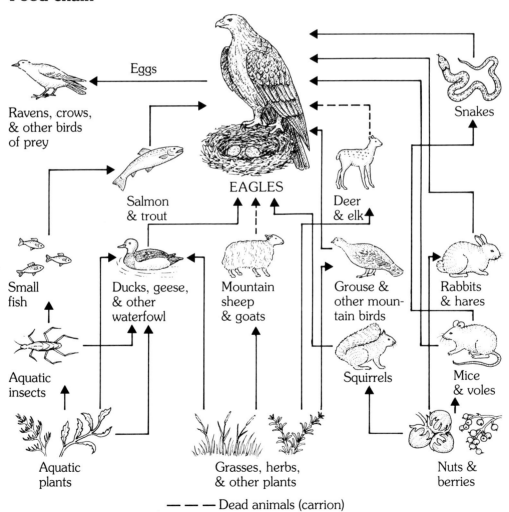

Ravens, crows, & other birds of prey

Eggs

EAGLES

Snakes

Salmon & trout

Deer & elk

Small fish

Ducks, geese, & other waterfowl

Mountain sheep & goats

Grouse & other mountain birds

Rabbits & hares

Aquatic insects

Squirrels

Mice & voles

Aquatic plants

Grasses, herbs, & other plants

Nuts & berries

— — — Dead animals (carrion)

The knowledge that all life is connected may help save eagles for future generations to enjoy.

Other predators, including hawks and falcons, wildcats, foxes, wolves, and bears, share the eagles' place at the top of a food chain. When poisons get into our *environment*, predators at the top of a food chain suffer the most, because the poisons build up and become more concentrated as they travel through the chain from plants to small animals. Predators that eat these animals get the strongest dose of all and often become ill and die.

Fortunately, people are now beginning to realize how important these food chains are to the life on our planet. Knowing that all forms of life are connected is important in protecting our environment. We must also be sure to protect the wild mountain countryside where eagles like to live. For it is only in these rugged, open places — well away from human disturbance — that eagles can flourish. Here is where they have the freedom to hunt for food and rear their young in safety — and where we can still see them as they soar high above the earth. We have an obligation to respect and protect all wild things that share the Earth with us.

Glossary and Index

These new words about eagles appear in the text on the pages shown after each definition. Each new word first appears in the text in *italics*, just as it appears here.

Reading level analysis: FRY 4.5, FLESCH 87 (easy), RAYGOR 5.5, FOG 6, SMOG 3

Library of Congress Cataloging-in-Publication Data

Scott, James A., 1946-
    The eagle in the mountains / words by Jim Scott ; photographs by Wendy Shattil & Bob Rozinski of Oxford Scientific Films.
       p. cm. -- (Animal habitats)
    Includes index.
    Summary: Text and photographs depict eagles feeding, breeding, and defending themselves in their natural habitats.
    ISBN 0-8368-0113-X
    1. Eagles--Juvenile literature. [1. Eagles.] I. Shattil, Wendy, ill. II. Rozinski, Robert, ill. III. Oxford Scientific Films. IV. Title. V. Series.
QL696.F32S36   1989
598'.916--dc20   89-4461

North American edition first published in 1989 by Gareth Stevens, Inc., 7317 West Green Tree Road, Milwaukee, WI 53223, USA
Text copyright © 1989 by Oxford Scientific Films. All rights reserved. No part of this book may be reproduced in any form or by any means without permission in writing from Gareth Stevens, Inc.
Conceived, designed, and produced by Belitha Press Ltd., London.
Consultant Editor: Jennifer Coldrey. Art Director: Treld Bicknell. Design: Naomi Games. US Editor: Mark J. Sachner. Line Drawings: Lorna Turpin.

The author and publishers wish to thank the following for permission to reproduce copyright material: **Wendy Shattil and Robert Rozinski** for pp. 1, 2, 3, 6, 7, 8 both, 9 both, 10 both, 11 both, 12 both, 13, 14, 15, 16 both, 17, 20 both, 21, 22 both, 23, 24 both, 25 both, 26, 27 below, 28 both, 29, 31, and front and back covers; **Oxford Scientific Films Ltd.** for pp. 4 above (Animals Animals — Stouffer Enterprises Inc.), 4 below (Roy Coombes), 5 both (Stan Osolinski), 18 (Animals Animals — Philip Hart), 19 above (Animals Animals — Charles Palek), 19 below (Animals Animals — Harold E. Wilson); p. 27 above is courtesy of the Denver Museum of Natural History, Denver, Colorado.

Printed in the United States of America
1 2 3 4 5 6 7 8 9 95 94 93 92 91 90 89
For a free color catalog describing Gareth Stevens' list of high-quality children's books call 1 (800) 433-0942